Welcome!

Are you ready to get your novel up and running?

No matter where you're starting from, planning a novel is a simple process… if you have a process.

Without a process it's *hard*.

Simple doesn't necessarily mean easy though, but this workbook provides the process and space to get it all in order.

All you need to do is fill in the blanks and build your chapter by chapter outline. Simple.

Inside you'll find all the questions you need to help you understand your story, and the templates necessary to hit all the major story points for outlining your novel from beginning to end.

When you're done planning, use it as your 'once source of truth' reference book.

Good luck!

Your opinion matters to me!

Please let me know what you think of this workbook by leaving a review where you purchased it.

If you have any improvements you'd like to see, email your ideas to Chris@ChrisAndrews.me

Enjoy!

Chris

Using This Workbook

This workbook is a companion to *Character and Structure: An Unholy Alliance,* which delivers all the core knowledge professional storytellers use for developing and troubleshooting stories - and shows you how to use it.

You don't have to have read *Character and Structure: An Unholy Alliance* to use this workbook, but you'll certainly get more out of it if you have.

If you already have a solid understanding of storytelling you're good to go. If not, grab a copy of C&S or do a little research to clarify anything you're not sure about.

This workbook is easy enough for anyone with a basic grasp of storytelling to use, yet in-depth enough to provide everything you need to outline a complex novel.

Although this workbook is based around a simple process, you don't have to be a slave to it. Feel free to repurpose anything you like. It's your workbook, after all.

Otherwise, it's a handy place to keep your ideas together, and it makes for a great teaching aid.

That's it. It's time to get started.

Simply fill in the blanks and you'll soon have a well-planed and outlined novel.

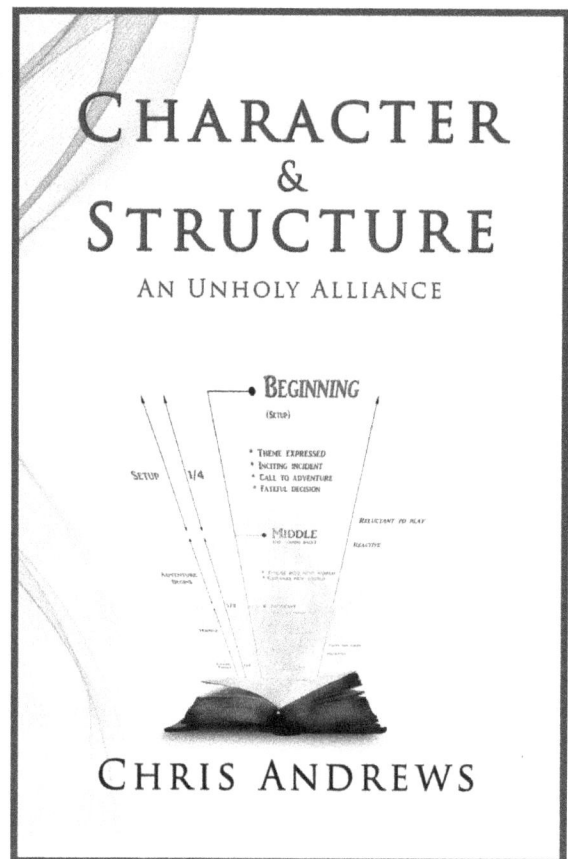

Assumptions

All novels differ in tone, theme, genre, length, number of chapters, scenes etc.

Because of that I've had to make some assumptions which may or may not fit every possibility. To add flexibility I've added extra sections with indicative headings you can use in any way you like.

Assumption 1. The number of chapters in any novel can vary greatly, but I've allowed for 40 (with space for more - or other notes - as you need it).

Assumption 2. You already have a good grasp of storytelling from reading *Character and Structure* or through your own research. Because of that, I'm assuming the terms used within aren't a mystery to you. It's not hard to look them up though.

Good luck! I'm looking forward to hearing about your success!

Novel Structure Diagram

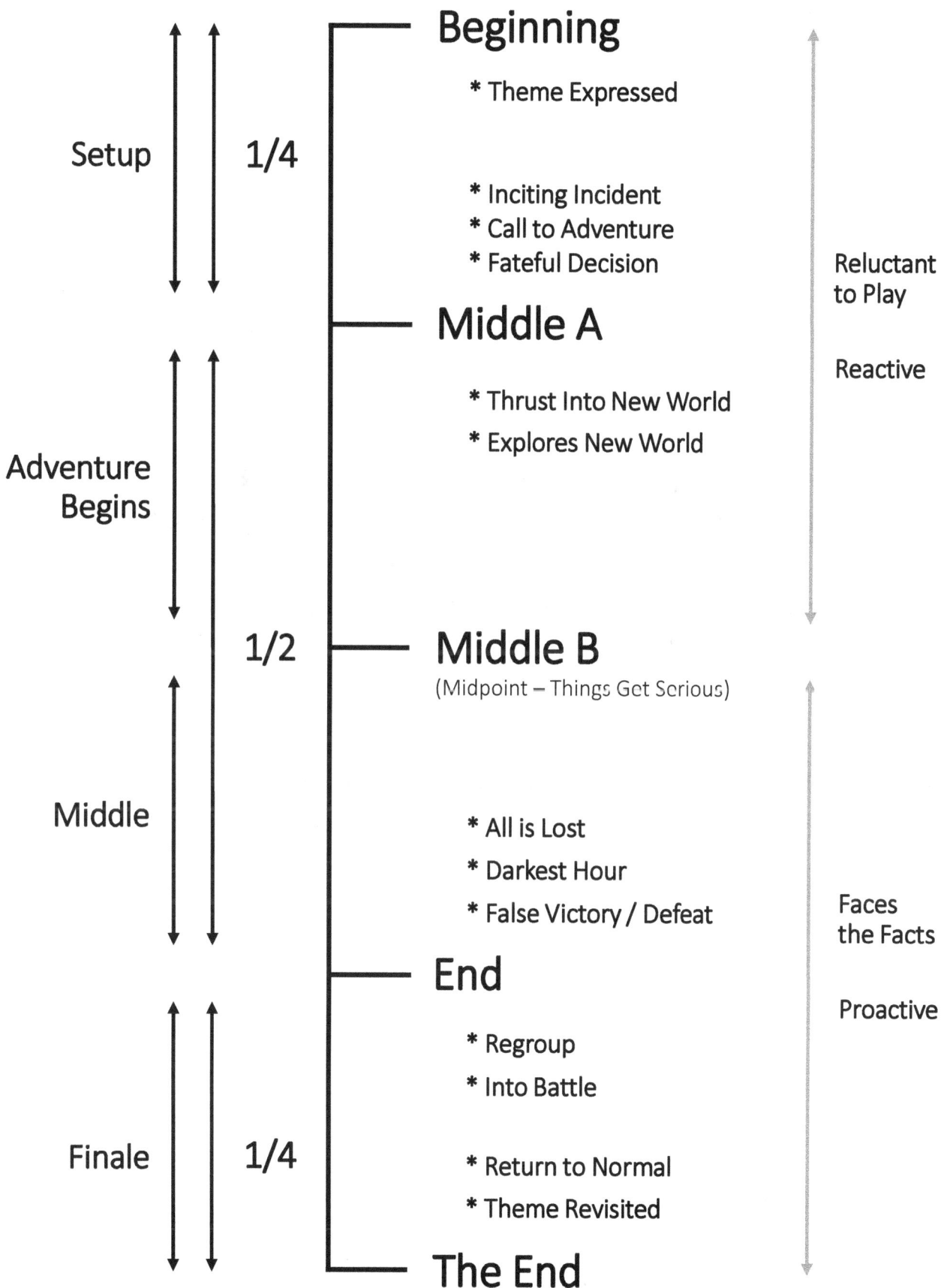

Setup — 1/4 — **Beginning**

* Theme Expressed

* Inciting Incident
* Call to Adventure
* Fateful Decision

Middle A

* Thrust Into New World
* Explores New World

Reluctant to Play

Reactive

Adventure Begins — 1/2 — **Middle B**
(Midpoint – Things Get Serious)

Middle

* All is Lost
* Darkest Hour
* False Victory / Defeat

End

* Regroup
* Into Battle

Faces the Facts

Proactive

Finale — 1/4

* Return to Normal
* Theme Revisited

The End

Part 1

Pre-Writing Questions

The Pre-Writing questions are often difficult to answer, but perhaps the most important part of planning a story.

This is because they give you insight into the kind of story you want to write and what's important to you, rather than the story itself.

This creates a level of depth that goes well beyond the plot to give your story more meaning.

Overview

Working Title:

Subtitle:

In general terms describe the story you want to write:

Primary Character List

(for easy reference)

Describe your characters so people will care about them

Name:
Details:

Name:
Details:

Name:
Details:

Name:
Details:

Name:
Details:

Name:
Details:

Name:
Details:

Name:
Details:

Name:
Details:

Name:
Details:

Name:
Details:

Name:
Details:

'You' Questions

How do you feel about your story?

What excites you about it?

'You' Questions

Why do you want to tell it?

Why do you care?

'You' Questions

What are you trying to make other people feel?

When someone finishes your story, how do you want people to react?

'You' Questions

How are you going to engage your audience's emotions?

What issues are you going to address that will affect their feelings?

'You' Questions

How are you going to make your audience care about your characters and what happens to them?

Other ideas or notes:

Questions About Your Theme

Theme: Write down several topics you care about. The more controversial or polarising, the greater the emotional impact.

Theme: Turn your preferred topics into statements or questions. I.e. 'Slavery is wrong!'

Name your preferred topic and statement to be your theme.

Story Problem Questions

What is the main story problem?

What else is worth fighting for (resources, ideals, power, etc?)

Story Problem Questions

What are the consequences for your story world if your protagonist fails to resolve the main story problem?

How will your protagonist resolve the story problem?

Story Problem Questions

What cool stuff happens? Think promo/book trailer moments.

Other ideas or notes:

Questions About Your Protagonist

What consequences will your protagonist face if they fail to resolve the main story problem?

Why do they care about the consequences (why is it personal)?

Questions About Your Protagonist

What do they want? This is external, like saving their friend or ending tyranny.

What do they need? This is internal, like courage or belief.

Questions About Your Protagonist

What does your protagonist need to do to satisfactorily resolve the problem?

Other ideas or notes:

Questions About Your Antagonist

What does your antagonist need to do to satisfactorily resolve the story problem for themselves?

What consequences do they face if they fail?

Questions About Your Antagonist

What will be the results if your antagonist succeeds? Ie, becomes Evil Overlord?

What will be the consequences for larger story world if your antagonist succeeds?

Structural Questions

What questions will your story raise in the first half?

How will your story answer the questions raised in the first half?

Structural Questions

What holds your protagonist back in the first half?

Why does your protagonist become proactive in the second half?

Structural Questions

What does your protagonist learn in the first half that will help them in the end?

How (specifically) do they apply what they've learned in order to succeed?

Story Opening Questions

Who are your main characters (in order of appearance if you can)?

How will you introduce them in the context of the story?

Story Opening Questions

How will you let your audience know what's unique or special about your story world?

How will you introduce your story's main problem?

Middle and Ending Questions

The middle educates your protagonist and equips them to win.
What specific lessons will you use to educate your protagonist (and other characters)?

How will you demonstrate these lessons in the context of the story?

Middle and Ending Questions

How will your protagonist use what they've learned to win?

Other ideas or notes:

Part 2

Story Structure Questions

The story structure questions need to be answered from a character perspective.

When viewed through the eyes of your characters, you gain insight into why the plot matters.

Inciting Incident

What are you going to introduce, remove, or foreshadow in your story world during the inciting incident?

How does the inciting incident affect the story?

Inciting Incident

How does your protagonist act or react?

Write down an idea for a scene that will demonstrate the inciting incident.

Call to Adventure

Which character calls your protagonist to adventure? Describe the situation.

Why do they do it?

Call to Adventure

What are the consequences of saying no?

What are the consequences of saying yes?

Call to Adventure

Write down an idea for a scene that will demonstrate the call to adventure.

What characters are involved?

Fateful Decision

What decision does your protagonist make in order to define their adventure?

What are the costs of their decision?

Fateful Decision

What are the potential rewards?

What decision would your ideal audience member make in the same circumstances?

Thrust Into New World

Your protagonist is now outside their comfort zone.
What has changed for your protagonist?

How do they deal with it?

Explores New World

What are you going to reveal to your protagonist about their story world?

How will you reveal these things?

Explores New World

How will this knowledge benefit the protagonist?

What is your protagonist going to learn about themselves or the world?

Explores New World

How are they going to feel about it?

Why are these things important to your story?

Midpoint

What change demonstrates things are getting more serious?

What is the first thing your protagonist does to demonstrate they're getting more proactive?

All is Lost

What plans, hopes or dreams did your protagonist expect to realise?

How are those plans, hopes or dreams destroyed at the all is lost moment?

The Darkest Hour

What event or realisation triggers the darkest hour for your protagonist?

What are the emotional consequences for your protagonist?

False Victory / Defeat

What are the conditions for a victory or defeat at this point of the story?

How will meeting or failing against these conditions affect the remainder of the story?

Regroup

What new plan does your protagonist come up with?

How do you plan to make this difficult?

Into Battle

What are they risking if they fail?

What has your protagonist learned up to this point that will help them 'win the battle'?

Into Battle

How exactly does your protagonist win?

What is the cost of winning (if anything)?

Into Battle

What does the antagonist lose?

Why will this win satisfy your audience?

Return to Normal

How has your protagonist changed?

How can you demonstrate how they've changed?

Theme Revisited

What has your protagonist learned that's indicative of your story's theme?

How will you show what they've learned?

Primary (Central) Storyline

Storyline summary (central plot):

Main points to include:

How will you introduce this storyline?

How will this storyline be resolved?

Additional Storylines

Subplot 1 (i.e., romance subplot)

Introduction:

Resolution:

How it contributes to Primary storyline:

Subplot 2 (ie, family issues subplot)

Introduction:

Resolution:

How it contributes to Primary storyline:

Subplot 3

Introduction:

Resolution:

How it contributes to Primary storyline:

Subplot 4

Introduction:

Resolution:

How it contributes to Primary storyline:

Subplot 5

Introduction:

Resolution:

How it contributes to Primary storyline:

Additional Storylines

Subplot 6

Introduction:

Resolution:

How it contributes to Primary storyline:

Subplot 7

Introduction:

Resolution:

How it contributes to Primary storyline:

Subplot 8

Introduction:

Resolution:

How it contributes to Primary storyline:

Subplot 9

Introduction:

Resolution:

How it contributes to Primary storyline:

Subplot 10

Introduction:

Resolution:

How it contributes to Primary storyline:

Rules for your story world

Your rules (you need at least 3) must:
- set boundaries
- influence the relationships between characters
- contribute to the underlying causes of your story's conflict

Rule 1

Rule 2

Rule 3

Rule 4

Rule 5

Rule 6

Rule 7

Rule 8

Rule 9

Rule 10

Part 3

Putting It Together

Now you have some insight into the direction you want to take your story and why, it's time to start assembling the foundations.

Don't be afraid to introduce new ideas or get creative at any point.

What you've written so far can easily be changed.

The Promise of the Premise

Describe (don't name) your protagonist in three words or less (ie, spoiled princess):

State what your protagonist wants (ie, to stop the Evil Overlord):

What's standing in their way? (the story's main conflict):

The hook, or the irony in the situation (ie, the Evil Overlord is their best friend):

Use the answers above to develop a one-sentence story premise using 25 words or less:

Halves

Genre:

Story Premise:

Primary Theme:
(Question or Statement)

Why will anyone care?

First Half:
(What happens?)

What problems
will be raised?

What questions
will be raised?

Second Half:
(What happens?)

How will you resolve
these problems?

How will you answer
these questions?

Unresolved problems
or questions for sequels?

Character & Structure Points

Place into chapters in order of appearance – the chapter numbers are a guide only.

Hook/opening image:
(Beginning - Chapter 1)

Theme expressed:
(Beginning - Chapter 1 or 2)

Call to Adventure:
(Beginning - Chapter 6-10)

Fateful Decision:
(Beginning - Chapter 9-10)

Thrust into New World:
(Middle A - The Adventure Begins.
How will they react?)

Explores New World:
(Middle A - Show Contrast With What
They're Familiar With)

All Is Lost:
(Middle B - Chapter 26-30)

Darkest Hour:
(Middle B - Chapter 26-30)

False Victory/Defeat:
(Middle B - Chapter 26-30)

Regroup:
(End - Chapter 31-35)

Into Battle:
(End - Chapter 32-38)

Return to Normal:
(End - Chapter 36-40)

Theme Revisited:
(End - Chapter 39-40)

1st Quarter Details

Describe how the story starts and how it leads to adventure:

2nd Quarter Details

Describe the beginning of the adventure and what your protagonist learns:

3rd Quarter

Describe how the tone changes and why 'things get serious':

4th Quarter

Describe how your protagonist goes for the win, and the outcome:

Beginning – Chapter Planner

Chapter 1:

Chapter 2:

Chapter 3:

Chapter 4:

Chapter 5:

Chapter 6:

Chapter 7:

Chapter 8:

Chapter 9:

Chapter 10:

Middle (A) - Chapter Planner

Chapter 11:

Chapter 12:

Chapter 13:

Chapter 14:

Chapter 15:

Chapter 16:

Chapter 17:

Chapter 18:

Chapter 19:

Chapter 20:

Middle (B) - Chapter Planner

Chapter 21:

Chapter 22:

Chapter 23:

Chapter 24:

Chapter 25:

Chapter 26:

Chapter 27:

Chapter 28:

Chapter 29:

Chapter 30:

The End – Chapter Planner

Chapter 31:

Chapter 32:

Chapter 33:

Chapter 34:

Chapter 35:

Chapter 36:

Chapter 37:

Chapter 38:

Chapter 39:

Chapter 40:

Extra Chapters or Scenes

Part 4

Scene-by-Scene Outline

If you need more scenes,
use the notes section at the back.

If you need to rearrange them,
change the scene numbers.

Chapter 1 – Outline

Primary Conflict:

Chapter overview:

Chapter 2 – Outline

Primary Conflict:

Chapter overview:

Chapter 3 – Outline

Primary Conflict:

Chapter overview:

Chapter 4 – Outline

Primary Conflict:

Chapter overview:

Chapter 5 – Outline

Primary Conflict:

Chapter overview:

Chapter 6 – Outline

Primary Conflict:

Chapter overview:

Chapter 7 – Outline

Primary Conflict:

Chapter overview:

Chapter 8 – Outline

Primary Conflict:

Chapter overview:

Chapter 9 – Outline

Primary Conflict:

Chapter overview:

Chapter 10 – Outline

Primary Conflict:

Chapter overview:

Chapter 11 – Outline

Primary Conflict:

Chapter overview:

Chapter 12 – Outline

Primary Conflict:

Chapter overview:

Chapter 13 – Outline

Primary Conflict:

Chapter overview:

Chapter 14 – Outline

Primary Conflict:

Chapter overview:

Chapter 15 – Outline

Primary Conflict:

Chapter overview:

Chapter 16 – Outline

Primary Conflict:

Chapter overview:

Chapter 17 – Outline

Primary Conflict:

Chapter overview:

Chapter 18 – Outline

Primary Conflict:

Chapter overview:

Chapter 19 – Outline

Primary Conflict:

Chapter overview:

Chapter 20 – Outline

Primary Conflict:

Chapter overview:

Chapter 21 – Outline

Primary Conflict:

Chapter overview:

Chapter 22 – Outline

Primary Conflict:

Chapter overview:

Chapter 23 – Outline

Primary Conflict:

Chapter overview:

Chapter 24 – Outline

Primary Conflict:

Chapter overview:

Chapter 25 – Outline

Primary Conflict:

Chapter overview:

Chapter 26 – Outline

Primary Conflict:

Chapter overview:

Chapter 27 – Outline

Primary Conflict:

Chapter overview:

Chapter 28 – Outline

Primary Conflict:

Chapter overview:

Chapter 29 – Outline

Primary Conflict:

Chapter overview:

.

Chapter 30 – Outline

Primary Conflict:

Chapter overview:

Chapter 31 – Outline

Primary Conflict:

Chapter overview:

Chapter 32 – Outline

Primary Conflict:

Chapter overview:

Chapter 33 – Outline

Primary Conflict:

Chapter overview:

Chapter 34 – Outline

Primary Conflict:

Chapter overview:

Chapter 35 – Outline

Primary Conflict:

Chapter overview:

Chapter 36 – Outline

Primary Conflict:

Chapter overview:

Chapter 37 – Outline

Primary Conflict:

Chapter overview:

Chapter 38 – Outline

Primary Conflict:

Chapter overview:

Chapter 39 – Outline

Primary Conflict:

Chapter overview:

Chapter 40 – Outline

Primary Conflict:

Chapter overview:

Additional Chapters / Scenes / Notes

Additional Chapters / Scenes / Notes

Additional Chapters / Scenes / Notes

Additional Chapters / Scenes / Notes

Additional Chapters / Scenes / Notes

Additional Chapters / Scenes / Notes

Additional Chapters / Scenes / Notes

Additional Chapters / Scenes / Notes

Additional Chapters / Scenes / Notes

Your opinion matters.

If you found this workbook helpful, please leave a review wherever you purchased it.

Reviews help others decide if something's right for them or not.

Thank you in advance.

Chris

The Novel and Script Planner Workbooks

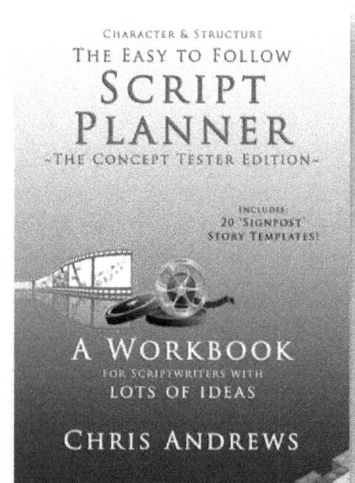

CHARACTER & STRUCTURE
THE EASY TO FOLLOW
NOVEL PLANNER
~TRILOGY EDITION~
INCLUDES:
THREE NOVEL TEMPLATES AND A
TRILOGY OVERVIEW SECTION!
A WORKBOOK
FOR OUTLINING A TRILOGY
CHRIS ANDREWS

CHARACTER & STRUCTURE
THE EASY TO FOLLOW
NOVEL PLANNER
~REGULAR EDITION~
INCLUDES:
THREE NOVEL
TEMPLATES!
A WORKBOOK
FOR OUTLINING UP TO
THREE NOVELS
CHRIS ANDREWS

CHARACTER & STRUCTURE
THE EASY TO FOLLOW
NOVEL PLANNER
~QUADRILOGY EDITION~
INCLUDES:
FOUR NOVEL TEMPLATES AND A
QUADRILOGY OVERVIEW SECTION!
A WORKBOOK
FOR OUTLINING
A FOUR-BOOK SERIES
CHRIS ANDREWS

CHARACTER & STRUCTURE
THE EASY TO FOLLOW
NOVEL PLANNER
~DEEP DIVE EDITION~
A WORKBOOK
FOR WRITERS WHO
NEED TO KNOW EVERYTHING
CHRIS ANDREWS

CHARACTER & STRUCTURE
THE EASY TO FOLLOW
NOVEL PLANNER
~FAST AND FREE EDITION~
20 TEMPLATES!
A WORKBOOK
FOR WRITERS WHO JUST
WANT TO GET ON WITH IT
CHRIS ANDREWS

CHARACTER & STRUCTURE
THE EASY TO FOLLOW
SCRIPT PLANNER
~METICULOUS VISION~
A WORKBOOK
FOR SCRIPTWRITERS WHO WISH THEY HAD
FORESIGHT
CHRIS ANDREWS

CHARACTER & STRUCTURE
THE EASY TO FOLLOW
SCRIPT PLANNER
~3 SCRIPT EDITION~
INCLUDES:
3 TEMPLATES!
A WORKBOOK
FOR OUTLINING UP TO
THREE SCRIPTS
CHRIS ANDREWS

CHARACTER & STRUCTURE
THE EASY TO FOLLOW
SCRIPT PLANNER
~THE CONCEPT TESTER EDITION~
INCLUDES:
20 'SIGNPOST'
STORY TEMPLATES!
A WORKBOOK
FOR SCRIPTWRITERS WITH
LOTS OF IDEAS
CHRIS ANDREWS

www.chrisandrews.me/workbooks

Stay in Touch

If you want to stay in touch, I have a blog where you can keep up to date and subscribe to my newsletter:

- http://www.chrisandrews.me

Wishing you the best of luck and success,

Chris Andrews

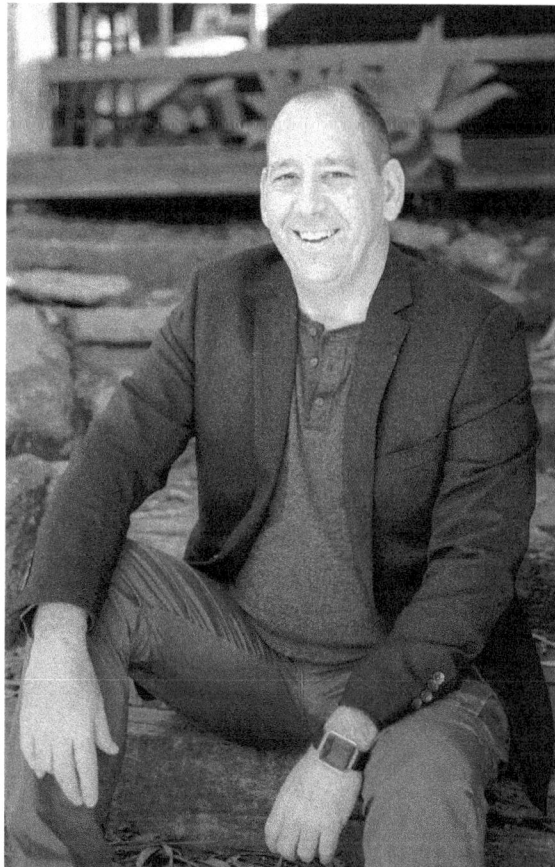

www.ingramcontent.com/pod-product-compliance
Lightning Source LLC
Chambersburg PA
CBHW080901030426

42335CB00019B/2417